THE BATTLE OF COWPENS

A Documented Narrative
and
Troop Movement Maps

Edwin C. Bearss

The Overmountain Press

JOHNSON CITY, TENNESSEE

Originally published by
Office of Archeology and Historic Preservation
National Park Service
U.S. Department of the Interior
October 15, 1967

ISBN 1-57072-045-2
Reprinted 1996 by The Overmountain Press
Printed in the United States of America

1 2 3 4 5 6 7 8 9 0

TABLE OF CONTENTS

Foreword v

Chapter I   Morgan Crosses the Broad 1

Chapter I   Notes. 6

Chapter II   Morgan Decides to Accept Battle
at the Cowpens 9

Chapter II   Notes. 23

Chapter III The Americans Rout Tarleton 27

Chapter III Notes. 47

Bibliography. 53

About the Author 57

LIST OF MAPS

I   Troop Movements of Phase I, January 17, 1781, from Daybreak to 7 a.m. 20

II   Troop Movements of Phase II, January 17, 1781, from the British Advance to the Withdrawal of Pickens' Militia 32

III Troop Movements of Phase III, January 17, 1781, from the Advance of the 71 (Fraser Highlanders) to Howard's Counterattack 38

IV Troop Movements of Phase IV, January 17, 1781, the Rout of the British. 42

FOREWORD

The Battle of Cowpens: A Documented Narrative and Troop Movement Maps was first printed for the National Park Service by Historian Edwin C. Bearss in October 1967, 186 years after the battle occurred. Originally written as a study document for the National Park Service, the book has since been used by other researchers, historians, and lay persons as they attempt to learn more about this battle.

What key ingredients are necessary to set the stage for dramatic results in battle? Thorough research is the best way of determining the factors which led men like Morgan and Tarleton to make the decisions they did.

Who were these men and what life experiences led them to this spot in the back country of South Carolina in January 1781? Who were the men under their command? Composed of the regular Continental line, sharpshooters, militia, dragoons, well-seasoned veterans, and raw recruits, they all shared a common interest that cold morning, of defeating their enemy. The defeat of the British heralded a resounding shout throughout the camps of the patriot cause for freedom. It was a victory much needed by a struggling nation.

The name "Cowpens" has been a part of the National Park Service since March 9, 1929. However, it was the push of our nation's upcoming bicentennial in 1976 that led to the expansion and protection of the battlefield proper in the early 1970s.

We are pleased The Overmountain Press has decided to reprint this manuscript; and I am proud to be associated with this acknowledgment of the role Historian Ed Bearss played in documenting the story. It is a fitting tribute to the battle story and to the author, but most of all to the men who fought this battle on a bitter Wednesday morning, January 17, 1781.

Patricia A. Ruff
Chief Ranger, Cowpens NB

CHAPTER I
Morgan Crosses the Broad

"Seldom has a battle, in which greater numbers were not engaged, been so important in its consequences as that of Cowpens," wrote John Marshall.

The annihilation of Major Patrick Ferguson's corps at Kings Mountain on October 7, 1780, by the "backwatermen" had stalled for the time being the British campaign aimed at the subjugation of North Carolina. Spirits that had been dampened by the crushing defeat inflicted on Major General Horatio Gates by the British at Camden in August soared.

In early October, the Continental Congress directed General George Washington to designate an officer to replace Gates as commander of the Southern Army. Washington moved promptly, and he named Major General Nathanael Greene as Gates' replacement.[1]

Greene reached Charlotte, North Carolina, on December 2, where on the following day, Gates formally turned over to him command of the Southern Army.[2] The first tasks of the new commander would be to restore discipline and to provision his troops. When he reached Charlotte, he learned from Gates that there were but three days' provisions on hand in the magazines. To make the situation more embarrassing, the region had been stripped of surplus food and forage by the army.

General Greene soon learned from his chief engineer, Thaddeus Kosciuszko, that the region on the Pee Dee River, near Cheraw Hill, was unravaged by war and could subsist the army. But as Cheraw Hill was farther from Lord Charles Cornwallis' base at Winnsboro than Charlotte, a march to that point would be interpreted as a retreat by the Patriots. Greene would therefore have to take some action to encourage the South Carolina partisan bands led by Francis Marion, Thomas Sumter, and Andrew Pickens. To meet this situation, Greene made a daring decision: he would divide his army. As his critics would point out, in event of disaster, this decision was opposed to the established rules of warfare. Military writers held that to divide an inferior force in the face of a superior enemy was to invite destruction in detail of one's forces.

On the other hand, there were compelling reasons to disregard the classic rule. First, Greene saw that by separating his army, it would be easier for both to subsist on the country, drawing rations and forage from regions where the British obtained their supplies. Second, if Cornwallis advanced against Greene's right wing, the left might threaten Charleston; if against the left wing, the British posts at Ninety-Six and Augusta would be endangered. As to the danger of either wing being attacked and mauled, Greene relied on the mobility of the Americans to outdistance the slow moving British infantry columns.[3] Thus, Greene had matured the only scheme of operations from which he could hope for success.

General Greene confirmed Brigadier General Daniel Morgan in the command of the light infantry, now composed of 320 Maryland and Delaware Continentals, 200 Virginia militia under Major Triplett, and "from 60 to 100" light dragoons under Lieutenant Colonel William Washington. This would constitute one of the two wings into which the army was to be divided; the other was entrusted to Brigadier General Isaac Huger. Greene would march with Huger's wing.[4]

On December 16 Greene notified Morgan, "You are appointed to the command of a corps of Light Infantry, a Detachment of Militia, and Lieutenant Colonel Washington's Regiment of Light Dragoons." With this force he was to proceed to the west side of the Catawba River, where he was to be reinforced by a body of North Carolina militia led by Brigadier General William Davidson, and by the militia lately led by General Sumter. This force would be employed "either offensively or defensively" against the foe west of the Catawba.

His mission would be to afford protection to that part of "the country and to spirit up the people—to annoy the enemy in that quarter—collect the provisions and forage out of the way of the enemy."

Should the British march toward the Pee Dee, where Greene proposed to take position, Morgan was to move in "such direction as to enable you to join me if necessary, or to fall upon the flank or into the rear of the enemy, as occasion may require."[5]

Hard rains that flooded the lowlands delayed Greene's departure, but on December 20 General Huger put his column in motion. The march was very difficult: the roads were ribbons of mud, the horses were too weak from lack of forage to pull the wagons without frequent halts, and the soldiers not much better off. On the 26th the left wing reached Cheraw Hill and camped.[6]

Morgan's command of approximately 600 left Charlotte on December 21, the day after Greene's column had started for Cheraw Hill, and reached the Catawba River that evening, and the next morning crossed the river at Biggin's Ferry. Pushing on by way of Cane Creek, Morgan's troops crossed the Broad on the 24th, and on Christmas went into camp on the left bank of the Pacolet, at Grindall's Ford.[7] Here Morgan was joined, a few days later, by a party of mounted militia under Colonel Pickens and Lieutenant Colonel James McCall.[8] General Davidson reported to Morgan on the 29th with 120 Whigs whom he had recruited in Mecklenburg. Leaving Major James McDowell in charge of the North Carolina militia, Davidson hurried off to bring into the field 500 more whom he had enrolled. Before he could return, however, the battle had occurred.[9]

On December 27, Morgan learned that about 250 Georgia

Tories had advanced to Fair Forest. To rout this force, he ordered out Colonel Washington's troopers and 200 mounted militia under Colonel McCall. The Tories retired in face of Washington's advance, but after a hard ride of 40 miles they were overtaken on the 28th at Hammond's Storehouse. Washington attacked immediately and scattered the Tories with great loss. Although at considerable distance from any supporting force, and within range of the British strongholds at Ninety-Six and Winnsboro, Washington moved against Fort Williams, 15 miles northeast of Ninety-Six. The British commander abandoned the post, and Washington, perceiving the wisdom of withdrawing, returned to the Pacolet.[10]

The action at Hammond's Store goaded Lord Cornwallis into action. He realized that Greene had made a wise move in dividing his army. Cornwallis knew that it would be a mistake to move with his entire force against Greene, because it would leave the posts at Ninety-Six and Augusta open to attack by Morgan, nor could he assail Morgan without leaving Greene free to march on Charleston. The situation was not only embarrassing, but it was made extremely irritating by the raids of the American partisans. Lord Cornwallis realized that to cope with this situation he would have to divide his force. His favorite cavalry officer, Lieutenant Colonel Banastre Tarleton, was ordered to Ninety-Six with his British Legion. Orders were issued for Major General Alexander Leslie to march upon Camden, while he with the main column would advance from Winnsboro up the watershed separating the Broad and Pee Dee rivers.[11]

Tarleton broke camp at the beginning of January and crossed the Broad with his Legion, the 1st Battalion, 71st (Fraser's Highlanders), and one 3-pounder. By the time he had pushed 20 miles beyond Brierly's Ferry, Tarleton had satisfied himself that Colonel Washington had pulled back from Fort Williams and that Ninety-Six was not endangered. He therefore determined to bring up his baggage train, which he had left at the ferry, camp, and make certain recommendations to Lord Cornwallis regarding how to cope with Morgan and Greene. He saw that Cornwallis could not afford to begin another invasion of North Carolina with Morgan in position to hit his exposed flank, and, brushing it aside, sweep down on Ninety-Six. Consequently, he proposed to force Morgan into battle, or, failing in that, to drive him over Broad River, where Cornwallis, sweeping up the left bank, could pocket him.

Cornwallis was impressed and agreed to reinforce Tarleton with 200 men of the 7th Fusiliers, 50 of the 17th Light Dragoons, and a few artillery men with another light 3-pounder. The addition of these units would give Tarleton a striking force of nearly 1,100 effectives. Colonel Tarleton as soon as he was reinforced moved out. Since he had tremendous self confidence and little respect for the Patriots' fighting ability, he expressed no concern when Major Newmarsh told him that most of the 200 men in his 7th Fusiliers were recruits.[12]

As the rivers and streams were running bank full as a result of recent rains, Tarleton's column experienced considerable difficulty in effecting a crossing of Indian and Duncan creeks. Meanwhile, his scouts and spies kept track of Morgan's movements. They reported that Morgan was being constantly reinforced. Tarleton accordingly forwarded a message to Lord Cornwallis, asking that he be allowed to retain the 7th Fusiliers. Cornwallis was agreeable. Upon receipt of this information, Tarleton resumed his march toward the northwest on the 12th. He hoped by this move to locate fords to facilitate the passage of the Enoree and Tyger by his infantry. As Tarleton's column pushed toward the source of these rivers, Cornwallis' army was feeling its way forward from Winnsboro. He had been compelled to slow his pace to allow General Leslie, then struggling through the swamps along the Pee Dee, to get into position.[13]

CHAPTER I—Notes

1. Christopher Ward, *The War of the Revolution*, 2 vols. (New York, 1952), Vol. II, 748. Greene, since early in the war, had been Washington's right arm. In the opinion of some military historians, Greene, both as a strategist and as a tactician, was Washington's superior.

2. The army, at this time, had a paper strength of 90 cavalrymen, 60 artillerists, and 2,307 infantrymen. Of the infantry, 949 were Continentals. *Ibid.*,749.

3. *Ibid.*, 749-751.

4. *Ibid.* Daniel Morgan was born in Hunterdon County, New Jersey, in 1736. Having moved to Virginia in 1753, he was commissioned a captain of Virginia riflemen in June, 1775. He participated in the expedition against Quebec, where he was captured. Released in 1776, he was commissioned colonel. In 1777 he was at Saratoga. He resigned from the army in 1779, but he returned to the service after the battle of Camden, and soon thereafter he was made a brigadier general. Colonel Washington was the son of Bailey Washington of Virginia.

5. Theodorus Bailey Myers, *Cowpens Papers, Being a Correspondence of General Morgan and Prominent Actors* (Charleston, 1881), 9-10.

6. Ward, *War of the Revolution*, II, 752.

7. H.L. Landers, *Historical Statements Concerning Battle of Kings Mountain and Battle of Cowpens, South Carolina*, 70th Congress, 1st Session, House Document No. 328 (Washington, 1928), 59; David Schenck, *North Carolina, 1780-81, Being a History of the Invasion of the Carolinas by the British Army under Lord Cornwallis* (Raleigh, 1889), 200. Biggin's Ferry was just below the mouth of the South Fork.

8. Schenck, *North Carolina*, 200.

9. Myers, *Cowpens Papers*, 30-31. General Davidson was from Rowan County. Major McDowell of "Quaker Meadows" had reported to Morgan with 190 riflemen from Burke County. Schenck, *North Carolina*, 200.

10. Landers, *Historical Statements*, 59-60. Fair Forest was about 20 miles south of Grindall's Ford.

11. John W. Fortescue, *A History of the British Army*, 13 vols. (London, 1902), Vol. III, 356-357. Tarleton was born in Liverpool on August 21, 1754, and was not yet 27 years old. His appearance is familiar to collectors of history in the large mezzotint engraving of his portrait by Sir Joshua Reynolds, representing him as a dashing cavalry officer with his foot raised on a cannon while adjusting his boot top, a position severely criticized, as exposing "the best part of his person," by Colonel de Chamilly, a partisan officer with whom he quarreled on technical matters. Myers, *Cowpens Papers*, 29. The British Legion numbered, at this stage of the conflict, 550 effectives, part dragoons and part mounted infantry, many of whom had been in Gates' army before its rout at Camden. They had been talked into joining the Legion by promises of food, arms, and clothing. Kenneth L. Roberts, *The Battle of Cowpens: The Great Morale Builder*, (New York, 1958), 59.

12. Banastre Tarleton, *A History of the Campaign of 1780 and 1781 in the Southern Provinces of North America*, (Dublin, 1786), 212-213. The 7th Fusiliers had been slated to garrison Ninety-Six.

13. *Ibid.*, 213; Henry Lee, *Memoirs of the War in the Southern Department of the United States* (New York, 1869), 225.

CHAPTER II
Morgan Decides to Accept Battle at the Cowpens

On January 14, 1781, General Morgan learned that Tarleton's column had crossed the Tyger at Musgrove's Mill. Until this moment, he had planned to resist the crossing of the Pacolet. But he was concerned by the reports brought in by his scouts that Lord Cornwallis was getting into position to threaten his left and rear. A successful defense of the Pacolet, he realized, would be "attended by no other important result, than to give Cornwallis time to gain his rear: while a defeat, under such circumstances," would be disastrous. For guidance he reviewed General Greene's instructions of December 29 which called for him to hold his ground as long as possible, but gave him the discretion of retreating if the security of his command were threatened. When he questioned his scouts, they warned him that the Pacolet was fordable in many places, and as such he would be courting disaster should he attempt to hold it. In addition, his men had stripped the area of forage for their livestock and of ham and hominy for themselves, so that supplying his army was becoming a problem. Yet if he pulled back, it would curb the ardor of the Whigs living in the district, and subject them to harassment by the Tories. Although Cornwallis' advance was snail-like, Morgan knew if he delayed much longer, he might be left with only two options—to fight a greatly superior force or to withdraw into the mountains.

Morgan accordingly determined to pull back from the Pacolet and take position nearer the upper fords of the Broad. Then if he were compelled to fight, he would be closer to the reinforcements of militia known to be en route to join him. Should Cornwallis remain where he was, Morgan, once he had been reinforced, would take the offensive against Tarleton. If compelled to retreat by Cornwallis' continued advance up the left bank of the Broad, Morgan planned to make for the area drained by the Catawba, where his gain would be three-fold: (a) it was a region not yet ravaged by war; (b) the militia of that area could be expected to rally to his standard; and (c) the way would be opened to a junction of his wing with Greene's army.[1]

While Morgan was mulling over his next move, his thoughts were rendered academic by news that Tarleton was sweeping toward Grindall's Ford. Word was now received that Cornwallis' army was advancing up the left bank of Broad River "like Bloodhounds" after prey. Satisfied that the movements of the British were directed against him, Morgan broke up his camp and pulled back ten miles to Burr's Mill on Thicketty Creek, where he camped on the afternoon of the 15th. Patrols were left to watch the Pacolet fords.[2]

Growing more anxious by the moment, Morgan wrote Greene on the evening of the 15th, telling of Tarleton's approach and reminding him that rations were scarce. It was impracticable "to procure more provisions in this quarter than was absolutely necessary for our own immediate consumption," he complained. Indeed, there were so many horses to be fed that the "most plentiful country must soon be exhausted." Nothing he could accomplish would equal the risk he faced by remaining in upper South Carolina. He requested that Greene recall his command, and that Generals Davidson and Pickens be left with their North and South Carolina militia to cow the Tories, as Tarleton was not likely to waste his time and energy on such a force. As Morgan was concluding his letter, he learned that Tarleton's column consisted of from 1,100 to 1,200 British regulars.[3] At this time, a courier was galloping across country with a dispatch from Greene to Morgan, dated the 13th. In it Greene had written,

"Col. Tarleton is said to be on his way to pay you a visit. I doubt not but he will have a decent reception and a proper dismission."[4]

Tarleton's corps had crossed the Enoree and Tyler, on the 14th, by using footlogs for his infantry and swimming his horses. That evening Tarleton learned from his scouts that Morgan's patrols were picketing the crossing of the Pacolet. Shortly thereafter, an express rider galloped into camp with a message that Cornwallis' army had reached Bulls Run and that General Leslie's command, although slowed in its march by rain-swollen streams and river, had finally emerged from the swamps. This message which Cornwallis had drafted on the 14th conveyed no information regarding Morgan's whereabouts beyond the fact that he did not believe he could recross the Broad, although it had crested and was falling.[5]

Before retiring for the night, Tarleton dashed off a message to his superior, assuring him that he would endeavor to pass the Pacolet. On doing so, he would compel Morgan to retire toward the Broad. Cornwallis in the meantime, he assumed, would be pushing up the east side of that river. If they moved with celerity the British might destroy Morgan's rapidly growing command.[6]

On the evening of the 15th, Tarleton resumed his advance. His initial goal was the ironworks located near the source of the Pacolet. The patrols, which Morgan had left to watch the crossings of the Pacolet, quickly pinpointed the British column. They followed the redcoats upstream several miles, and when Tarleton's people camped, the scouts did likewise. As soon as the Patriots had settled down for a good night's sleep, Tarleton turned out his Light Infantry Battalion. Moving swiftly and silently, they secured a crossing at unguarded Easterwood Shoals, within six miles of Morgan's camp at Burr's Mill. Tarleton now turned out the rest of his corps, putting them in motion to the bridgehead.

While his soldiers were fording the Pacolet, Tarleton's far-ranging scouts pinpointed a number of log cabins constructed by Major Ferguson's ill-fated command, about three miles to his front. As it was reported that these cabins were unoccupied, Colonel Tarleton determined to organize a flying column to secure them. A strong force of dragoons and mounted infantry moved out to discharge this mission, as the last of the rear guard was reaching the left bank of the Pacolet. Tarleton planned to post his command at the cabins and wait for Morgan to disclose his intentions.

The flying column had not been gone very long, before several excited scouts galloped up and reported that the Americans had hurriedly evacuated their encampment. Orders were issued for the flying column to occupy and hold the abandoned Burr's Mill camp. Upon reaching Burr's Mill, the British found that it was a strong position. Of greater interest to the enlisted men was the discovery that the Americans had pulled back so fast that they had left a large quantity of half-cooked rations behind.[7]

Morgan's scouts, as soon as they learned that they had been hoodwinked, raced for Burr's Mill to alert their General.[8] Thus, Morgan was warned of the danger at an early hour on January 16. He shouted for his men to turn out and to start loading wagons. Soldiers, who were preparing their breakfasts around the camp fires, scrambled to their feet, and soon the units had been formed and were ready to move. Morgan set out in the direction of Broad River, his troops eating their half-cooked rations as they went. He pushed them hard, shouting commands to the teamsters and the infantry, while Washington's cavalry watched the flanks and rear. The road along which the column marched was rough; several swamps had to be crossed. After passing Hancocksville, he turned the vanguard into a byroad that skirted the head of Thicketty Creek.[9]

There was no question about it, but on the morning of the 16th Morgan and his army were running for their lives. The one thing that Morgan could not risk was having Tarleton's cavalry overtake him while he was withdrawing. In his retreat Morgan had the counsel of his most able officers—Colonel William Washington, Major Giles, and Baron de Glaubec. He had the advice of Patriot spies and guides whose information had so far been reliable.

So through the 16th, Morgan weighed the odds with his guides and officers. During the early afternoon a messenger arrived from General Pickens, who had collected a detachment of mounted infantry and had crossed Broad River, and was en route to join Morgan. Meet him where? Pickens didn't say, and Morgan had to know where. Now there was one place in that wild region that was known to every Patriot guide in the Carolinas. That was the Cowpens, because the 3,000 backwoods militia that had rendezvoused in the preceding October to trap Major Ferguson had assembled there, before starting for Kings Mountain. The leader of the North Carolina militia under Morgan, Major McDowell, had been one of those to meet at the Cowpens. Pickens knew the place well. Morgan had to have a place of assembly that Pickens could not miss, even on the darkest night, a place to fight, a place to forage. So Morgan made up his mind, "we'll go to the Cowpens."[10]

Prior to this decision on Morgan's part, he had voiced a desire to cross the Broad, but dusk found the little army at Cowpens. With Pickens' militia en route to the designated rendezvous and the Broad five miles away and darkness at hand, Morgan did not wish to chance crossing a rain-swollen river with the British hard on his heels.[11]

The place where General Morgan established his camp on the night of January 16 was near the intersection of the Mill Gap road and the road from present day Spartanburg running northeast into North Carolina, and crossing Broad River at Island Ford. The Mill Gap road crossed the Broad at Cherokee Ford and ran northwestwardly into the mountains. Its route followed generally the ridge lines, thereby avoiding the crossing of the watercourses. Morgan's camp was in a wooded ravine, about 1,000 yards northwest of the cabin of Robert Scruggs, which was visited in 1849 by B. J. Lossing.[12]

For years the stockgrowers, which comprised a large portion of the population of upper South Carolina, had been in the habit of grazing their cattle in this area before driving them to the coast to market. The area was forested with red oaks, hickory, and pines. As it was heavily pastured, there was no undergrowth. The site where Morgan halted was known locally as Hannah's Cowpens from its owner.[13]

Morgan knew he would have to fight here, if Tarleton overtook him that night or early the next morning. The open woods would give Tarleton room to maneuver his cavalry, and there were no swamps or thickets to protect the Americans' flanks. It was "certainly as proper a place for action as Colonel Tarleton could desire," wrote Tarleton in his *Memoirs*. "America does not produce many more suitable to the nature of the troops under his command."[14]

Subsequently, Morgan was criticized because of his choice of ground. When he offered a defense, he failed to recall that he had originally planned to oppose Tarleton east of the Broad. Stoutly defending himself he wrote:

> I would not have had a swamp in the view of my militia on any consideration; they would have made for it, and nothing could have detained them from it. And, as to covering my wings, I knew my adversary, and was perfectly sure I should have nothing but downright fighting. As to retreat, it was the very thing I wished to cut off all hope of. I would have thanked Tarleton had he surrounded me with his cavalry. It would have been better than placing my own men in the rear to shoot down those who broke from the ranks. When men are forced to fight, they will sell their lives dearly.... Had I crossed the river, one half of the militia would immediately have abandoned me.[15]

Morgan, while he might have wished to meet the foe on the other side of Broad River, was not afraid to engage Tarleton at the Cowpens. He was a fighter by nature, utterly unafraid of physical danger. William Washington, a fearless officer himself, wrote that he had never seen a man more collected in time of danger than Morgan. The burly ex-teamster had supreme confidence in himself as a battlefield commander—even when his units included militia. A former militiaman, he had led such troops before. Moreover, the Southern frontier militia equated his activities with light infantry and the hit-and-run operations they preferred. They considered Morgan one of them; he too was a backwoodsman and had the speech and manners of the frontier. In the autumn of 1780 two large detachments of southern militia had asked permission to serve under him; one, the group that destroyed Ferguson's force at Kings Mountain.[16] A contingent of these Kings Mountain veterans were with Morgan now; they were Davidson's North Carolinians, serving under Major McDowell.

At the same time, Tarleton's successes, while they demonstrated that he was fearless, showed that he could be reckless, especially if he underestimated his foe. He had the cavalryman's dash, but he lacked the bull dog tenacity of the successful army commander. He was especially effective in the pursuit and seemed to be aroused by the flight of an enemy. While Morgan held his ground, Tarleton was as circumspect in his movements as any prudent officer could wish. But the moment Morgan appeared to flee before his column, he forgot all caution, as well as the need to coordinate his movements with Lord Cornwallis.[17]

On the night of his arrival at the Cowpens, Morgan was joined by Colonel Pickens, who, after being briefed, excused himself and soon returned with 150 militia from north of the Broad. Other militia, he reported, were en route to the point of danger. Many of these could be expected to arrive before morning. Morgan, unlike many of the American officers, appreciated the ability of these men as partisan fighters. He knew they were crack marksmen. With the exception of the Virginia militia, however, they could not be counted on to stand up and hold their ground in face of a bayonet charge by British regulars. Such was not the case with Morgan's other units. His infantry under Lieutenant Colonel John E. Howard was "the flower of the gallant brigade of Marylanders," who at Camden had rolled back the British left wing at the point of the bayonet. Colonel Washington's cavalry corps was well-known for its effectiveness. The members of the Virginia militia were combat tested veterans, who, having served one or more enlistments in the Continental Army, had been called out in the emergency that had followed the Patriots' rout at Camden.[18]

Word that Morgan had decided to give battle at the Cowpens took the army by surprise. Preparations proceeded accordingly. First, Morgan moved to strengthen his mounted arm. The formidable array of horse soldiers which Tarleton was about to hurl against the Americans made an increase in the size of the cavalry a matter of first importance. A call for volunteers went out. Fifty-six men stepped forward. As soon as they were issued sabers and pistols, they were organized into a cavalry corps of two companies—one led by Lieutenant Colonel James McCall and the other by Major Jolly. This battalion was to be commanded by Colonel McCall, as senior officer, who would look to Colonel Washington for orders.[19]

Morgan ordered the militia to make certain they had a sufficient supply of ammunition (24 rounds prepared and ready for use), and arrangements were made to send the baggage train to the rear. Scouts moved out to watch the foe and to warn against a surprise attack. Couriers thundered off with instructions to hurry forward any militia encountered. While the troops bedded down, Morgan met with his principal subordinates to lay plans for the battle.[20]

Morgan made an impression on the militia that remained with them for years. Thomas Young of Jolly's company recalled:

> We were very anxious for battle, and many a hearty curse had been vented against General Morgan during that day's march for retreating, as we thought, to avoid a battle. Night came upon us, yet much remained to be done. It was upon this occasion that I was more perfectly convinced of General Morgan's qualifications to command militia than I had ever before been. He went among the volunteers, helped them fix their swords, joked with them about their sweethearts and told them to keep in good spirits, and the day would be ours. Long after I laid down, he was going about among the soldiers, encouraging them, and telling them that the "Old

Wagoner" would crack his whip over Ben (Tarleton) in the morning, as sure as he lived. "Just hold up your heads boys," he would say, "three fires, and you are free! And then, when you return to your homes, how the old folks will bless you, and the girls kiss you, for your gallant conduct." I don't think that he slept a wink that night.[21]

Although he was half-crippled with the sciatica and rheumatism that had plagued him since the beginning of the campaign, Morgan seemed omni-present as he visited the units. To stimulate the "summer soldiers and sunshine patriots," Morgan coined the sign and countersign for the night, "Fire" and "Sword."[22]

At an hour before dawn, Morgan was apprised of Tarleton's advance by his pickets. "Tarleton is only five miles away!" they shouted.

"Boys get up!" Morgan roared, "Benny is coming."[23]

Within a few moments, the camp was astir. Breakfast had been prepared the night before, and now Morgan told his men to eat hearty. The baggage wagons rolled to the rear, amid a cracking of whips. While the officers were forming their units, the mounted militia was told to tie their horses in the area behind the camp, where the wagons had been parked.[24]

The position Morgan had chosen for the battle lay to the right and left of the Mill Gap road, just southwest of the camp. The ground was slightly undulating. Two knolls topped the ridge along which the Mill Gap road ran. Morgan's main line of resistance would be located on the knoll southwest of the hollow, in which the camp was established. To its front for 300 yards there is a scarcely perceptible slope downward; beyond this the slope is greater, dropping off into a shallow ravine 700 yards from the main line of resistance. To the rear of the principal position, and west of the camp was the second knoll slightly higher than the first. This knoll continues across the Mill Gap road in a south and southwest direction, but at a slightly less elevation. The ground offered no cover for either belligerent, except such as was provided by the trees. The flanks of both armies would be exposed, as the terrain was favorable in all directions for troop movements.[25]

Morgan, in making his dispositions to receive Tarleton's onslaught, exhibited a keen understanding of the strength and weaknesses of the troops involved. He would make the best use of the firepower of his militia without compelling them to stand up against the foe in hand-to-hand combat.

Morgan's battle plan was to employ the Maryland and Delaware Continentals and Virginia militia as his shock troops. Near the brow of the first slope, he posted his best troops, Colonel Howard's battalion of light infantry—280 combat-ready veterans. Howard's center company was astride the Mill Gap road. Major Triplett's company of Virginia militia and Captain Beaty's company of South Carolina militia were deployed on Howard's right.[26] On the Continentals' left were positioned about 100 Augusta riflemen of Virginia led by Captains Tate and William Buchanan.[27] Colonel Howard was placed in tactical command of the 400 men holding Morgan's main line of resistance.

One hundred and fifty yards down the face of the slope, skillfully positioned in the grass and among the trees, Morgan stationed 300 Georgia, and North and South Carolina militia. These troops, many of them expert riflemen, were formed in extended order and posted to guard the flanks. Colonels Brannon and Thomas with their South Carolina militia were on the extreme right, while Major McDowell and his North Carolinians were between the road and the South Carolinians. Colonel Hammond with part of Colonel McCall's regiment of South Carolina State Troops was posted east of the road. To Hammond's left was Captain Donnolly and his Georgians. Colonel Pickens would be in overall command of these units.[28]

As soon as the militia had taken position in the open woods, Major McDowell, accompanied by about 60 picked marksmen from his command, and Major John Cunningham, with a like number of Georgia sharpshooters, advanced about 150 yards and took position as skirmishers—Cunningham's people on the left and McDowell's on the right.[29]

Behind these three lines and concealed by the second knoll, Morgan held in reserve 80 dragoons under Colonel Washington. Colonel McCall with his and Major Jolly's companies (about 40 effectives), which had been outfitted as dragoons, were formed east of the road and 100 yards to the left of Washington's people. McCall would look to Washington for his orders.[30] In rear of the cavalry, the horses of the militia were picketed in a grove of young pines. They were saddled and bridled, ready for instant use.[31] Captains Inman and Price with their mounted companies were advanced down the Mill Gap road, with orders to keep a sharp lookout for the British vanguard.[32]

Morgan's disposition of his troops was unorthodox. The most unreliable American units were in front, well in advance of the Continentals. But Morgan knew his militia, and he told his officers how he proposed to use this formation to beat Tarleton. His directions were simple. To the skirmishers of the first line he said, "Let the enemy get within killing distance"—or about 50 yards—then blaze away, especially "at the men with epaulets." After this the skirmishers could retire, "seeking shelter from the trees, as opportunity might offer, loading and firing until they reached Pickens' line, which they were to join." Morgan knew his skirmishers would take to their heels, and this was his way of showing them how to do it—but effectively and without panic.[33] The deployment of the skirmishers, the left wing of Georgians and the right of Carolinians, was adopted by Morgan with the view of arousing a spirit of rivalry, which might add to the men's effectiveness. "Let me see," Morgan remarked, "which are most entitled to the credit of brave men, the boys of Carolina or those of Georgia."[34]

After being joined by the skirmishers, Pickens' militia would hold their fire until the redcoats approached to within 50 yards. Then, after delivering two well-directed volleys, they were to retire in good order, and take position on the left of the Continentals, firing by regiment as they withdrew.

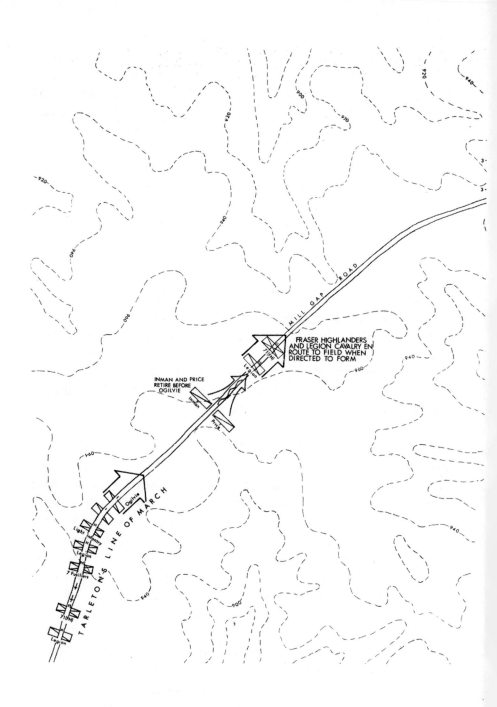

FRASER HIGHLANDERS
AND LEGION CAVALRY EN
ROUTE TO FIELD WHEN
DIRECTED TO FORM

INMAN AND PRICE
RETIRE BEFORE
OGILVIE

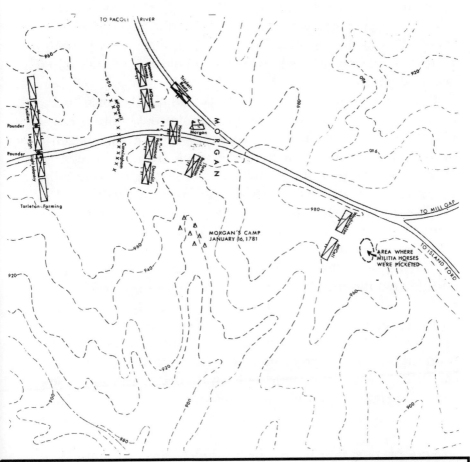

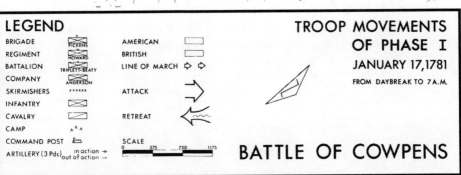

Here they would be reformed and held in reserve. He then made a fiery speech which was calculated to bolster the militia's self confidence. As he pounded his fist into his palm, he remarked that he expected to see them display their usual zeal and courage.

Morgan's words to the Continentals and militia constituting his main line of resistance were understandably brief. These troops did not need the "stimulus of spirit-stirring speeches to fit them for the performance" of their duty. He prepared them for the retreat of the militia, by repeating the orders he had given that portion of his command. They were told to fire low and deliberately, not to break for any reason, and if compelled to retreat, to rally on the knoll to their rear.

Orders were dispatched for Colonel Washington to assist in rallying the militia in case they broke, and to cover them should they be pursued. In addition, he was to protect the horses of the militia, and to hold himself ready to act as circumstances might dictate. The hillock occupied by the cavalry was well-chosen. The knoll to their front, and the gradual descent beyond it, screened them from the fire of the British, without obscuring from them a horseman's view of the battlefield for some distance in front of the main line of resistance. It provided, besides, a secure rallying point for the militia.

Every preparation having been made, Morgan established his command post in rear of the Continentals, and confidently awaited the approach of the redcoats.[36]

Chapter II—Notes

1. James Graham, *The Life of General Daniel Morgan of the Virginia Line of the Army of the United States...* (New York, 1859), 281-283; William Johnson, *Sketches of the Life and Correspondence of Nathanael Greene, Major General of the Armies of the United States in the War of the Revolution,* 2 vols. (Charleston, 1822), I, 372.

2. Graham, *Morgan,* 283; Don Higginbotham, *Daniel Morgan—Revolutionary Rifleman* (Chapel Hill, 1961), 129.

3. Morgan to Greene, Jan. 15, 1781, in Graham's *Morgan,* 285-28

4. Greene to Morgan, Jan. 13, 1781, in Graham's *Morgan,* 275.

5. Robert D. Bass, *The Green Dragoon* (New York, 1957), 149; Cornwallis to Tarleton, Jan. 14, 1781, in Tarleton's *Campaigns,* 248. The Enoree and Tyger were crossed above the Cherokee road.

6. Tarleton, *Campaigns,* 213.

7. *Ibid.,* 213-214.

8. Graham, *Morgan,* 284.

9. *Ibid.*; Joseph Johnson, *Traditions and Reminiscences, Chiefly of the American Revolution in the South* (Charleston, 1851), 449.

10. Roberts, *Battle of Cowpens*, 65-68. Major Giles was Morgan's chief aide-de-camp, while Baron de Glaubec was his volunteer-companion. *Ibid.*, 61.

11. Memoir of Thomas Young, in Johnson's *Traditions and Reminiscences*, 449; Graham, *Morgan*, 284.

12. Landers, *Historical Statements*, 63.

13. Hugh F. Rankin, "Cowpens: Prelude to Yorktown," *North Carolina Historical Review*, Vol. XXXI, No. 3, p. 353.

14. Tarleton, *Campaigns*, 221.

15. Johnson, *Greene*, I, 376.

16. Higginbotham, *Daniel Morgan*, 132-133.

17. Graham, *Morgan*, 289.

18. *Ibid.*, 290.

19. Memoir of Thomas Young, in Johnson's *Traditions and Reminiscences*, 451. Major Jolly's company was from the Union District of South Carolina. Young served in Jolly's company.

20. Graham, *Morgan*, 291-292; "Memoir of Thomas Young, a Revolutionary Patriot of South Carolina," *The Orion*, III (Oct., 1843), 88.

21. "Memoir of Thomas Young," 88.

22. Roberts, *Battle of Cowpens*, 74.

23. Rankin, "Cowpens: Prelude to Yorktown," 355.

24. "Memoir of Thomas Young," 88; Graham, *Morgan*, 293.

25. Landers, *Historical Statements*, 63-64; S. Hammond, in Johnson's *Traditions and Reminiscences*, 527-528.

26. Graham, *Morgan*, 295; Morgan to Greene, Jan. 19, 1781, in Graham's *Morgan*, 468; Hammond, in Johnson's *Traditions and Reminiscences*, 527-530. The left of the Triplett-Beaty battalion was to be opposite Howard's right, but 100 yards in its rear; "its right extending toward the foe, so as to be opposite or parallel with the second line."

27. *Ibid.* The Augusta riflemen's left wing was pulled back about 100 yards to the rear of Howard's right flank, and their left was thrown forward, "so as to bring it nearly parallel" with the Continentals' left.

28. Graham, *Morgan*, 211-212; Hammond, in Johnson, *Traditions and Reminiscences*, 527-530; Morgan to Greene, Jan. 19, 1781, in Graham's *Morgan*, 467-470. Morgan reported that McDowell was on the right and Cunningham on the left, while Colonels Brannon and Thomas of the South Carolinian militia were posted on McDowell's right, and Colonels Hays and McCall of the same corps were on Cunningham's left. Colonel Hammond of the South Carolinian militia reported that from right to left Pickens' line was held by Cunningham, McDowell, Hammond, and Donnolly. As Hammond made his notes at the time of the deployment, I feel that his report is more accurate as he was more intimately connected with the South Carolinian militia than Morgan.

29. Graham, *Morgan*, 295-296; North Callahan, *Daniel Morgan, Ranger of the Revolution* (New York, 1961), 211-212.

30. Graham, *Morgan*, 295-296; Hammond, in Johnson's *Traditions and Reminiscences*, 527-530.

31. Graham, *Morgan*, 296.

32. Hammond in Johnson's *Traditions and Reminiscences*, 527-530.

33. Graham, *Morgan*, 297; George F. Scheer and Hugh F. Rankin, *Rebels and Redcoats* (New York, 1957), 430.

34. Graham, *Morgan*, 297.

35. *Ibid.*, 297-299.

36. *Ibid.*, 299.

CHAPTER III
The Americans Rout Tarleton

After halting at Burr's Mill late on the afternoon of January 16, 1781, Colonel Tarleton dispatched patrols and spies to observe the movements of Morgan and his people. The 17th Light Dragoons were directed to follow the foe till dark, while spies were to question people known for their Whig sympathies as to what they might know about Morgan's intentions.

It was after dark before Tarleton received his first reports. A patrol had watched the Americans as they "struck into byways," leading toward Thicketty Creek. Not long thereafter, a party of Loyalists brought in an American Colonel of Militia who had strayed from his unit. Tarleton questioned the Colonel. The information gained, along with other reports collected by his men, satisfied Tarleton that his proper course of action would be to hang "upon General Morgan's rear, to impede the junction of reinforcements, said to be approaching, and likewise to prevent his passing Broad river without the knowledge of the light troops...."

About midnight, Tarleton was awakened to receive a report that a "corps of mountaineers" were on the march from Green River to join Morgan. This added to the urgency of the situation—the Americans would have to be watched closely, if he were to capitalize on any mistakes Morgan might make.[1]

Tarleton was so eager to fulfill his boast to destroy Morgan's corps or push it back against Kings Mountain, where Lord

Cornwallis could finish it off, that he allowed his men little rest on the night of the 16th. At 3 a.m. on January 17, 1781, Tarleton called in his pickets, and the British took up the march.[2] The redcoats followed the route taken by the Americans the preceding evening, as they had pulled back to the Cowpens. Since he would travel light and fast, Tarleton left his baggage and wagons behind. The troops, detailed from each unit of the corps to guard the train, were to follow the main column at daybreak.

As the column moved out in the darkness, three companies of light infantry, supported by the Legion infantry, took the advance. The 7th Fusiliers, the Royal Artillerists with their two 3-pounders, and the 1st Battalion 71st (Fraser's Highlanders) constituted the main column; the cavalry and mounted infantry brought up the rear. Progress was slowed by the configuration of the terrain. Numerous creeks and ravines had to be crossed in the darkness. In addition, the men guarding the flanks had to move cautiously, because this was ambush country. Before dawn, Thicketty Creek was crossed. Tarleton now called a brief halt to let an advance guard of cavalry take the lead. An American patrol led by Captain Inman was encountered, pursued, and two of its members captured. The prisoners, when questioned, told the British that Morgan was camped five miles away. Whereupon, Tarleton ordered Captain Ogilvie of the Legion to the front with two companies of dragoons. The chase was not continued much farther before Captain Ogilvie sent word that the Rebels had halted and were forming for battle.[3]

Tarleton now called for and closely questioned his guides. These people, who were familiar with the area, explained that

the woods were open and free from swamps; that the part of Broad River, just above the place where King's creek joined the stream, was about six miles distant from the enemy's left flank, and that the river, by making a curve to the westward, ran parallel to their rear.[4]

Subsequently, Tarleton reported:

America does not produce many more suitable [fields for battle] to the nature of the troops under...[my] command. The situation of the enemy was desperate in case of misfortune; an open country, and a river in their rear, must have thrown them entirely in the power of a superior cavalry; whilst the light troops, in case of a repulse, had the expectation of a neighboring force to protect them from destruction.[5]

Tarleton accordingly was delighted with the situation. He believed he had Morgan just where he wanted him—with a rain-swollen river to his rear. In case of a repulse, Tarleton could look to Cornwallis and Leslie for assistance. He would attack immediately. Orders were given for the Legion dragoons to drive in the militia patrols covering Morgan's front, so the British could reconnoiter Morgan's position. Pressing forward on the Mill Gap Road, the Legionaries forced Captains Inman's and Price's scouts to pull back. Tarleton was now able to ascertain that the Americans had posted their troops in two lines—the front line, he estimated, to consist of about 1,000 militia and the second of 500 Continentals. After having studied the American position, Tarleton had his officers see that their men shucked their gear, except their arms and ammunition. The Light Infantry Battalion was filed to the left till its front equalled that of Pickens' militia posted east of the road.[6] The green-uniformed infantry of the British Legion filed into position on the left of the Light Infantry Battalion.[7] A 3-pounder, called a "grasshopper", was positioned between these two units.

Covered by the fire of the 3-pounder, these commands closed to within 300 yards of Morgan's skirmish line. Next, the 7th Fusiliers were advanced and formed on the left of the Legion infantry, while the other 3-pounder was emplaced along the right of the 7th Fusiliers.[8] A captain, each with 50 dragoons, was posted to the right and left of the infantry battle line. Besides guarding Tarleton's flanks, the dragoons would threaten those of the Americans. The 1st Battalion, 71st Infantry (Fraser's Highlanders) was ordered to form 150 yards to the rear and echeloned to the left of the 7th Fusiliers. The kilted Highlanders, along with 200 green-uniformed horsemen of the British Legion, were to constitute Tarleton's reserve.[9]

Tarleton, his fighting blood aroused, was so eager to close with the foe that he ordered the attacks before his officers could complete their dispositions. Major Newmarsh of the 7th Fusiliers was still posting his officers. The 1st Battalion, 71st Infantry and the cavalry had not disentangled themselves from "the brushwood with which...[Thicketty] Creek abounds" at the time they were directed to form and await orders.[10]

Astride his horse, behind Howard's Continentals, Morgan caught sight of green-jacketed dragoons riding among the trees at the far end of the slope, 400 yards in front of his skirmishers. They were followed by infantrymen in red and white. It was about 7 a.m., and the day was clear and cold. As the British gathered at the edge of the open woods, Tarleton sent a detachment of dragoons to scatter Morgan's skirmishers. Cunningham's Georgians and McDowell's North Carolinians obeyed their orders. As they retired on Pickens' line, they kept up a desultory but effective fire which unhorsed 15 of the British.[11] One section of the skirmishers merged with Pickens' militia, while the remainder circled and reformed in rear of Howard's Continentals.[12]

After the dragoons had been recalled, it was intended that McDowell's and Cunningham's people should resume their positions in front of Pickens' battle line. Before they could do so, Tarleton's artillery roared into action, under cover of which his right wing took up the advance.[13]

As drums rolled and fifes shrilled, the British "raised a prodigious yell and came running as if they intended to eat us up," Morgan recalled. "It was the most beautiful line I ever saw," commented Thomas Young of Jolly's cavalry:

> When they shouted, I heard Morgan say, "They gave us the British halloo, boys. Give them the Indian halloo, by God!" and he galloped along the lines, cheering his

men and telling them not to fire until he could see the whites of their eyes. Every officer was crying "Don't fire!" for it was a hard matter to keep us from it.[14]

Some of the recruits of the 7th Fusiliers lost their nerve and halted and opened fire. Their officers moved in, and after a few of the men had been knocked sprawling with the flat of a saber, they came to their senses. They then moved out "in as good a line as troops could move at open files."[15]

Covered by the fire of their artillery, the British drove to within 150 yards of Pickens' battle line, when the militia, at Pickens' command, let loose a deadly volley. A number of red-coats and green-coated legionaries were cut down, including several of the "epaulet men." The militia reloaded and fired again, staggering Tarleton's battle line. Being veterans, the British did not panic easily. They quickly dressed their ranks and pressed on, their bayonets at the ready. The militia, in accordance with Morgan's orders, now filed off toward the left end of Howard's line.[16]

Tarleton, seeing the militia take to their heels, sensed that victory was at hand. He ordered Captain Ogilvie, who commanded the 50 dragoons on the right, to charge the retreating Americans. By the time the hard-riding men of the 17th Light Dragoons thundered forward, the troops constituting Pickens' right had not passed from in front of Howard's line. Assailed by the dragoons they panicked, and instead of halting at Howard's line, they sought safety by fleeing toward the crest where Washington's cavalry was posted.[17]

Some of Pickens' militia ran fast enough to get to their horses and vanish. One of the militia officers was Lieutenant Hughes:

a man of great personal strength and of remarkable fleetness on foot. As [Hughes'] men, with others, broke...and fled before Tarleton's cavalry...with his drawn sword he would out-run his men and passing them, face about, and command them to stand, striking right and left to enforce obedience to orders; often

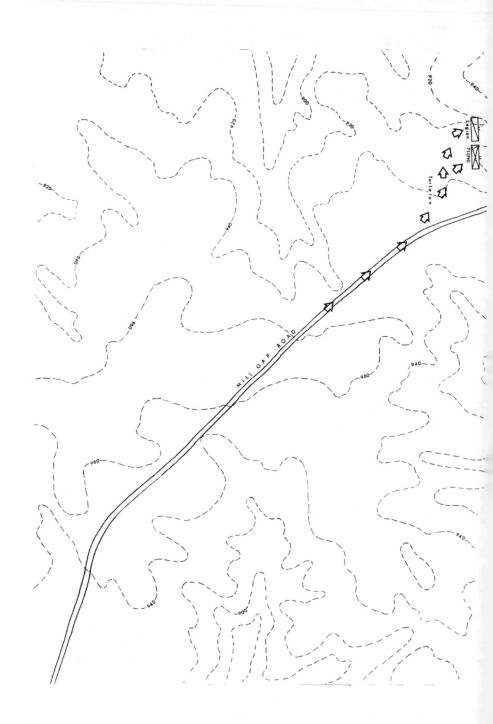

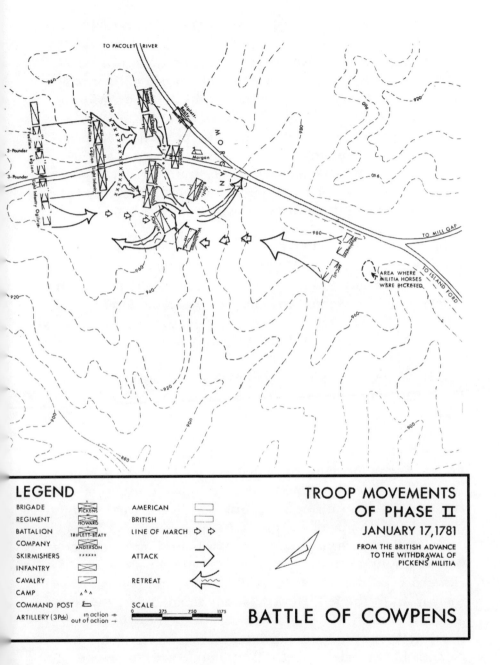

TO PACOLET RIVER

TO MILL GAP

TO ISLAND FORD

AREA WHERE
MILITIA HORSES
WERE PICKETED

LEGEND

BRIGADE		AMERICAN	
REGIMENT		BRITISH	
BATTALION		LINE OF MARCH	
COMPANY			
SKIRMISHERS		ATTACK	
INFANTRY			
CAVALRY		RETREAT	
CAMP			
COMMAND POST			
ARTILLERY (3Pdr)	in action out of action	SCALE	

TROOP MOVEMENTS
OF PHASE II
JANUARY 17, 1781

FROM THE BRITISH ADVANCE
TO THE WITHDRAWAL OF
PICKENS MILITIA

BATTLE OF COWPENS

repeating with a loud voice: "You damned cowards, halt and fight! If you don't stop and fight, you'll all be killed!" But most of them were for a while too demoralized to realize the situation or obey the commands of their officers. As they would scamper off, Hughes would renewedly pursue, and once more gaining their front, would repeat his tactics to bring them to their duty. At length the company was induced to make a stand, on the brow of a slope, some distance from the battle line, behind a clump of young pines that partially concealed and protected them from Tarleton's cavalry.[18]

Morgan saw the British horsesoldiers thunder forward, and he determined to commit his reserve—Colonel Washington's cavalry. As Ogilvie's dragoons rode among the Americans, Washington's horsemen struck them with such force that the British fled. Though Washington pursued them, Collins reported they were as hard to catch as a "drove of wild Choctaw steers."[19]

Meanwhile, Morgan had galloped to the end of Howard's line to rally the militia. While brandishing his sword and shouting encouragement to the last units to leave the field, he saw that many of the irregulars were heading for the area where their horses were tethered. Riding after them, he bellowed, "Form, form, my brave fellows...Old Morgan was never beaten." Assisted by Pickens, Morgan halted most of the militia, and the two officers began to re-form them behind Howard's main line of resistance.[20]

The British, believing that victory was in their grasp, let go a wild shout and advanced up the gentle slope against Howard's position. As soon as the militia had passed across their front to the left, Howard's men opened fire. A desperate fight ensued. For the better part of the next fifteen minutes, neither side gained an inch. Tarleton determined to commit his reserve. The 1st Battalion, 71st (Fraser's Highlanders) was to assail Howard's Continentals, while the cavalry threatened Morgan's right. The reserve at this time was about a mile away. Major Archibald McArthur of the Highlanders was told to pass the 7th Fusiliers before halting his men and having them blaze away. He was cautioned not to entangle his right with the left of the 7th. The cavalry of the British Legion, reinforced by the 50 dragoons posted to the left of the artillery, was to incline to the left, and to form a line, which would envelop the Americans' right.[21]

The Highlanders came forward on the double with their bagpipes skirling. The arrival of the Highlanders enabled the British to extend their left so that it overlapped Howard's right. Morgan at the same time saw that the British horse was getting ready to charge his endangered flank. Responding to this emergency with his characteristic alacrity, Morgan sent Colonel Brannon with instructions for Colonel Washington to regroup his troopers and to assail the foe before they could carry out their mission.[22]

After having taken this action, Morgan rode to the point of danger, where he found Colonel Howard badly shaken by the turn of events. Seeing that his right had been outflanked by the Highlanders, Howard decided that the best way to cope with this danger was by changing the front of his right flank company, Wallace's Virginians. Howard ordered Wallace's company to face about in line, then wheel to its left to form a right angle with the rest of the battle line, and thus be better able to oppose the advance of the Highlanders. This order was misunderstood, however. In executing it, the Virginia militia, after coming to the right about, marched forward and toward the rear, instead of wheeling to the right. Other officers along the line seeing this, and supposing that orders had been given for a retreat, faced their men about and moved rearward.

Morgan was understandably distressed by this development. Calling to Howard, he inquired, "Why are your men retreating?"

Howard replied, "I am trying to save my right flank."

"Are you beaten?"

"Do men who march like that look as though they are beaten?" Howard asked.

Morgan saw that the men were marching to the rear, as if

they were on parade. His confidence restored, Morgan told Howard to remain with his men until they reached "the rising ground near Washington's horse." He then rode ahead to select the "proper place for us to halt and face about."[23]

This was the climax of the battle and the crucial decision. If Morgan had panicked or not gone along quickly with Howard, the Cowpens would have had a different ending. As it was, the misunderstood order called for a lightning-like decision, an almost intuitive reaction. Daniel Morgan met the crisis superbly.

Tarleton's soldiers had seen the Continentals and Virginia militia start to retreat and assumed that victory was at hand. Shouting louder than ever in their eagerness to be in on the kill, the British dashed up the slope, breaking ranks. Colonel Washington, returning from his pursuit of Ogilvie and his dragoons, was to be right of the onrushing British, and he saw the confusion which had swept their ranks. "They are coming on like a mob; give them a fire and I will charge them," he messaged to Morgan.[24]

Howard's people had now reached the swale separating the knolls, and they had started up the hillock on which the cavalry had been posted at the beginning of the fight. Turning quickly on the retiring Continentals and Virginians, Morgan roared, "Face about, boys! give them one good fire,and the victory is ours!" He then galloped along the entire line.[25]

At this moment, the foe, confident of victory, was sweeping forward in an impetuous and disorderly fashion. As if on parade, the Continentals and Virginians faced about, and sent a volley crashing into the redcoats' ranks at a range of between 30 and 40 yards. Stunned by this unexpected and terrible fire, the British recoiled. Before they could recover from the shock, Colonel Howard called for a charge, and the grim Americans were upon them bayonets flashing. Tarleton, in the meantime, had called for his cavalry to charge. Just as the British horse was sweeping toward the foe, a volley crashed into their flank from an unexpected direction, and sent them reeling back in the wildest confusion. The dragoons of the Legion, ill disciplined at best, and spoiled by the easy successes Tarleton's dash had gained for them, were not the men to face a surprise attack.

Moments before, the British might have escaped by flight. But by this time Colonels Washington and Pickens were ready to strike. Washington's cavalry swept down upon Tarleton's right, while Morgan and Pickens hurled the re-formed militia at his left.[26]

The result was a double envelopment, perfectly timed. The British, Tarleton admitted, were thrown into a panic. Tarleton sent orders for his cavalry to rally and form about 400 yards to the right of the foe, while he endeavored to re-form the infantry to protect the two 3-pounders. The cavalry of the Legion, however, refused to listen to the pleas of their officers, while Tarleton's effort to collect the infantry was ineffectual. Neither promises nor threats could gain their attention. Many of the men of the 7th Fusiliers threw down their arms, and fell to the ground. Morgan watched as the Legion infantry and Light Infantry dropped their arms and accouterments and took to their "heels for security—helter-skelter." But they were quickly overtaken by the volunteer cavalry, and with the exception of a few, surrendered, about 200 yards from the point of disaster. As the Americans swept forward, the cry "Tarleton's Quarter" was raised. But a useless slaughter was avoided, as Morgan, Howard, and the other officers shouted for their men to spare their prisoners.[27]

As the Continentals forged ahead, Colonel Howard spotted the artillery a short distance to his front and called Captain Nathanial Ewing to take it. Captain Thomas Anderson of Delaware, hearing the order, also rushed for the same piece. Anderson won the race by placing "the end of his spontoon forward into the ground, made a long leap which brought him upon the gun and gave him the honor of the prize."[28] The other 3-pounder was captured by a detachment of Continentals led by Captain Robert H. Kirkwood.[29] Tarleton had watched in frustration as the Americans closed in on the handful of blue-coated Royal Artillerists. He sought to rally 250 dragoons of his Legion for a counterattack, for he felt that by a furious onset, he might yet win the day, as the

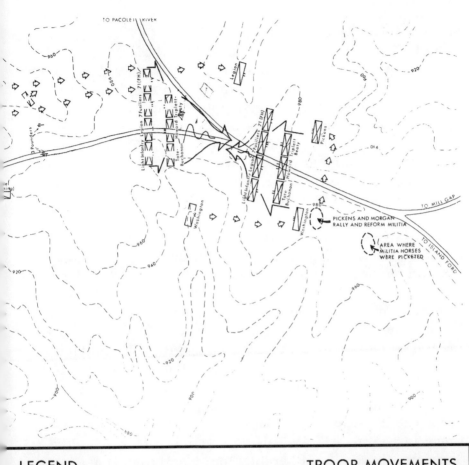

TO PACOLET RIVER

TO MILL GAP

TO ISLAND FORD

PICKENS AND MORGAN
RALLY AND REFORM MILITIA

AREA WHERE
MILITIA HORSES
WERE PICKETED

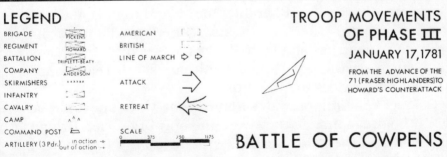

LEGEND

BRIGADE		PICKENS
REGIMENT		HOWARD
BATTALION		TRIPLETT-BEATY
COMPANY		ANDERSON
SKIRMISHERS	++++++	
INFANTRY		
CAVALRY		
CAMP	ᴧ ᴧ ᴧ	
COMMAND POST		
ARTILLERY (3 Pdr.)	in action	out of action

AMERICAN	
BRITISH	
LINE OF MARCH	⇨ ⇨
ATTACK	
RETREAT	

SCALE
0   375   750   1175

TROOP MOVEMENTS
OF PHASE III
JANUARY 17, 1781

FROM THE ADVANCE OF THE
71 (FRASER HIGHLANDERS) TO
HOWARD'S COUNTERATTACK

BATTLE OF COWPENS

Americans were badly disorganized by their sweeping success. He was unsuccessful, however. About 250 dragoons forsook their leader and rode off, bearing down any officer that opposed their flight.[30]

On the Americans' right, the battalion of the 71st had been able to hold Pickens' militia at bay. Deserted by their cavalry and fiercely assailed in front and on the flank by the militia, the Highlanders slowly pulled back. Just when it seemed as if they might escape, Colonel Howard, his Continentals freed by the quick surrender of the 7th Fusiliers, threw his right wing against them.

This movement threw their ranks into confusion. The militia rushed forward and engaged the Highlanders in hand-to-hand combat. Into the Scottish masses charged Colonel James Jackson at the head of his Georgians. He snatched at the regimental flag but missed. Howard promised quarter, and Major McArthur surrendered his sword to Colonel Pickens.[31]

Fourteen officers and 40 men of the 17th Light Dragoon rallied on Tarleton. As he led a charge in a futile effort to save the Highlanders, Tarleton was intercepted by Washington's cavalry. Tarleton's horse was shot from under him. Dr. Robert Jackson, Assistant Surgeon of the 71st, rode up and offered his horse to the Colonel. Tarleton refused, but Jackson insisted, exclaiming, "Your safety is of the highest importance to the army!" As Tarleton swung into the saddle, Jackson affixed a handkerchief to the end of his cane and walked toward the Americans. When challenged, he answered, "I am assistant surgeon of the Seventy-First. Many of the men are wounded and in your hands. I therefore come to offer my services to attend them."[32]

Colonel Washington was satisfied that Tarleton would be with the dragoons, as they were the only organized British force still on the field. Burning with desire to capture him, Washington ordered a pursuit. The Americans soon overtook the retreating foe, but in his eagerness to come to grips with the British, Washington had outdistanced most of his column. As Washington pounded into view, Tarleton and two of his officers wheeled their horses about. Undaunted, Washington struck at the first that approached him, the officer on Tarleton's right. Washington's sword crashed against the Britisher's and snapped off near the hilt. The English officer stood up in his stirrups to deal Washington a mortal blow. Just at this moment, a lad named Collins rode up and shot the Britisher in the shoulder. The uplifted arm fell. Tarleton's other companion moved to close with Washington, but he was routed by Sergeant-Major Perry. Tarleton pushed forward and made a thrust at Washington, which he parried with what remained of his sword. Tarleton, seeing that additional Americans were at hand, wheeled his horse around and rejoined his retreating dragoons. As he galloped off, he took a parting shot at Washington, whose horse received the ball.[33]

The detachment from each corps under Lieutenant Fraser of the 71st that was guarding the train received early news of the defeat from several Loyalists. He ordered the excess baggage destroyed, had the men climb into the wagons, and led them to Cornwallis' encampment. While on his forced march neither he nor any of his men saw any Americans or Colonel Tarleton's column. Fraser's command was the only infantry to escape the debacle.[34]

A body of Tories, who were attached to Tarleton's command and had been employed as guides and spies, moved in to plunder the abandoned wagons. Tarleton and his people came upon the Tories, and in their haste failed to ascertain their identity. Calling for a charge, Tarleton scattered the Tories, killing and wounding a number, before pushing on toward Broad River. Before reaching the Broad with the survivors of the disaster, Tarleton learned that Cornwallis had not advanced beyond Turkey Creek. He accordingly turned his column to the southeast toward Hamilton's Ford, where he could open direct communications with his superior.[35] About 200 horsesoldiers of the Legion, who had fled the field, reported to Tarleton on the 18th at Hamilton's Ford.[36]

A second party of dragoons, in addition to those with Tarleton, returned to the British lines, reporting in at Cornwal-

MILL GAP ROAD

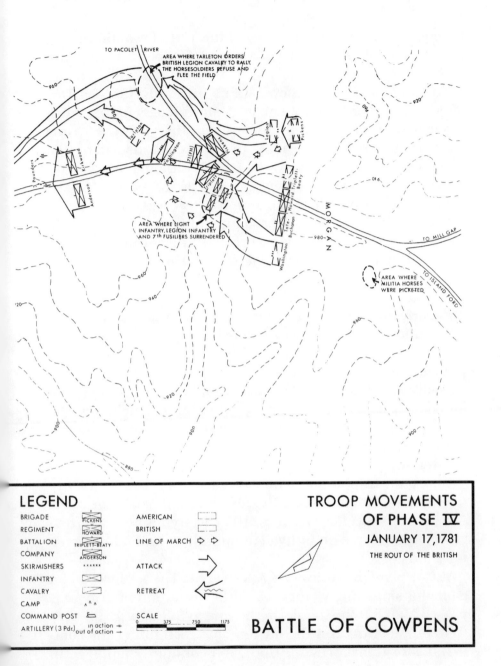

TO PACOLET RIVER

AREA WHERE TARLETON ORDERS
BRITISH LEGION CAVALRY TO RALLY.
THE HORSESOLDIERS REFUSE AND
FLEE THE FIELD

Pickens

Washington

71ST(H)

Legion

Triplett-Beaty

Howard

Kirkwood

Anderson

Pounders

Washington

Buchanon

AREA WHERE LIGHT
INFANTRY, LEGION INFANTRY
AND 7th FUSILIERS SURRENDERED

Washington

MORGAN

TO MILL GAP

TO ISLAND FORD

AREA WHERE
MILITIA HORSES
WERE PICKETED

LEGEND

BRIGADE		AMERICAN
REGIMENT	PICKENS	BRITISH
BATTALION	HOWARD	LINE OF MARCH
COMPANY	TRIPLETT-BEATY	
SKIRMISHERS	ANDERSON	ATTACK
INFANTRY	*****	
CAVALRY		RETREAT
CAMP	^ ^ ^	
COMMAND POST		SCALE
ARTILLERY (3 Pdr.)	in action	0 375 750 1175
	out of action	

TROOP MOVEMENTS
OF PHASE IV
JANUARY 17, 1781
THE ROUT OF THE BRITISH

BATTLE OF COWPENS

— 43 —

lis' encampment on the evening of the 17th. From these people, His Lordship first learned of the defeat of his young protégé.[37]

Washington and his troopers, in a futile effort to bag Tarleton, pressed on about 20 miles. Unfortunately for the Patriots' cause, they followed almost from the start the wrong road. They took a road leading to the Pacolet instead of that taken by the British toward the Broad. Although every effort was made, after the discovery of the error, to recover the lost time, the fugitives had too much of a headstart. On his return to the Cowpens, after abandoning the chase, Washington and his people swept through the countryside and rounded up about 100 stragglers from Tarleton's shattered corps.[38]

The battle had commenced about 7 a.m. and had continued for nearly an hour. Morgan listed his losses as: 12 killed and 61 wounded. This loss was chiefly sustained by the Continentals and Virginians, and particularly by the flank companies posted on the right of Howard's line. Tarleton lost 110 killed including one major, 13 captains, 14 lieutenants, and nine ensigns; 830 prisoners were counted, including 200 wounded. Tarleton had lost nine-tenths of his force; a fourth of Cornwallis' field army, a blow from which the latter never recovered.[39]

Among the trophies of victory were two stands of colors, two 3-pounders, 800 muskets, 35 wagons with the baggage of the 7th Fusiliers, 60 Negro slaves, 100 cavalry horses, one traveling forge, a large quantity of ammunition, and "all the enemy's music."[40]

At Cowpens on January 17, 1781, the Patriot forces had gained a smashing victory. Under a resolution of Congress passed March 9 the thanks of the United States were given to General Morgan, and the officers and men under his command, "for their fortitude and good conduct, displayed in the action at the Cowpens." The resolution further provided that a gold medal be presented to General Morgan, silver medals to Lieutenant Colonels Washington and Howard, and a sword to Colonel Pickens.[41]

News of the victory was welcomed by Patriots throughout the country. General Washington wrote the President of Congress on February 17 that he hoped this success would "check the offensive operations of the enemy until General Greene shall have collected a much more respectable force than he had under his command by the last accounts from him." The battle again proved the value, if employed properly, of the militia.[42]

Colonel Tarleton blamed his defeat on several factors: (a) the bravery and good conduct of the Americans; (b) "the loose manner of forming which had always been practiced by the King's troops in America; and (c) to the sudden onset which panicked his troops. The "extreme extension of the files" by the British, he continued, was responsible for the disaster. Previously, this had been nullified by the "multiplicity of lines with which the British generally fought. If infantry who are formed "very open, and only two deep," he wrote, "meet opposition, they can have no stability: But when they experience an unexpected shock, confusion will ensue, and flight, without immediate support, must be the inevitable consequence."[43]

One of Tarleton's subordinates, Lieutenant Roderick Mackenzie countered:

> if his [Tarleton's] files were too extended, why did he not contract them? For he says...that "the disposition was planned with coolness, and executed without embarrassment." Any other mode of attack, or disposition, therefore, which he might have planned, would doubtless have been executed with equal promptitude.[44]

Moreover, Mackenzie continued, Tarleton had been badly outgeneraled by Morgan. Because of his hurry to launch an attack, the advance had been taken up while the 7th Fusiliers was still forming and before the reserve had moved into its assigned position. Thus, the British infantry was in no condition to press its advance when the Continentals recoiled, as it had been exhausted by forced marches. Up till this moment, not less than two thirds of their officers had fallen. Morgan soon discovered that the Legion cavalry was holding back. He ordered Colonel Washington to cover Howard's people and to check the pursuit. Washington's dragoons carried out their mission, and Howard's infantry as soon as it had faced about launched a savage counterattack on the British. Mackenzie continued:

> In disorder from the pursuit, unsupported by the cavalry, deprived of the assistance of the cannon, which in defiance of the utmost exertions of those who had them in charge, were now left behind, the advance of the British fell back, and communicated a panick [sic] to others, which soon became general: a total rout ensued.[45]

Lord Cornwallis was understandably distressed. As a result of his experience at Camden, it seemed impossible that "an inferior force, two-thirds militia should gain such a decisive advantage over his favorite hero."[46]

Tarleton, in commenting on the disasters at Kings Mountain and Cowpens in his *Campaigns*, wrote that the defeat of Ferguson was a catastrophe which put an end to the first expedition into North Carolina, and the battle of Cowpens overshadowed the commencement of the second invasion. The battle of Cowpens greatly heartened the Patriots and cast a pall of gloom over the British army and their Tory sympathizers. It was a prelude to Yorktown.[47]

CHAPTER III—Notes

1. Tarleton, *Campaigns*, 214.

2. Lieutenant Mackenzie says the column moved out at 2 a.m.

3. *Ibid.*, 214-215; Bass, *Green Dragoon*, 153.

4. Tarleton, *Campaigns*, 215.

5. *Ibid.*, 221.

6. *Ibid.*, 215-216. The battalion of light infantry had a well-deserved reputation. The company of the 16th Regiment had served in General Augustine Prevost's army, while those of the 71st Regiment were "distinguished" under General William Grey at the surprise of General Anthony Wayne in Pennsylvania, "of Baylor's dragoons in New Jersey, at Briar Creek in Georgia, at the capture and subsequent defense of Savannah, at the battle near Camden...." Although only recently organized, the light company of the Prince of Wales' American Regiment had made a reputation under General William Tryon at Danbury. Roderick Mackenzie, *Strictures on Lt. Col. Tarleton's History "of the Campaigns of 1780 and 1781 in the Southern Provinces of North America"* (London, 1785), 112-113.

7. Tarleton, *Campaigns*, 215-216. Major General Sir Henry Clinton in the summer of 1778 had organized a mixed corps of infantry and cavalry of men recruited in America. One of these units was designated the British Legion to which Lord William Schaw Cathcart was named colonel. Tarleton was promoted to lieutenant colonel and joined the Legion, as its second in command. Cathcart was soon reassigned, and when the Legion sailed for the South in December, 1779, Tarleton was in charge. While in the South, the infantry of the British Legion had seen hard service, and in battle they had heretofore behaved well. Mackenzie, *Strictures*, 113.

8. Tarleton, *Campaigns*, 215-216. The 7th Fusiliers had served with credit from the beginning of the war. "Under General Clarke they had attained the summit of military discipline." Mackenzie, *Strictures*, 110.

9. Tarleton, *Campaigns*, 215-216. The 1st Battalion, 71st Regiment had landed in Georgia in 1778, and had made a reputation at Stone Ferry, the battle of Camden, and the sieges of Charleston and Savannah. Mackenzie, *Strictures*, Ill.

10. MacKenzie, *Strictures*, 99-100; David Ramsey, *The History of the American Revolution* (London, 1811), 233.

11. Graham, *Morgan*, 299; Rankin "Cowpens: Prelude to Yorktown," 356.

12. Thomas Anderson, "Journal of Lt. Thomas Anderson of the Delaware Regiment," *Historical Magazine*, 2d Series (April, 1867) 209.

13. Graham, *Morgan*, 299-300.

14. "Memoir of Thomas Young," 88.

15. Tarleton, *Campaigns*, 216. The advance was made in double rank at open files.

16. Graham, *Morgan*, 300.

17. *Private James Collins, Autobiography of a Revolutionary Soldier*, ed. John M. Roberts (Clinton, La., 859), 57.

18. Roberts, *Battle of Cowpens*, 89-90.

19. *Collins, Autobiography*, 57; Graham, *Morgan*, 301; Tarleton, *Campaigns*, 216; Mackenzie, *Strictures*, 98.

20. *Collins, Autobiography*, 57; "D. Wallace's History of Union...," Draper Papers, 13VV 188-189, State Historical Society of Wisconsin.

21. Tarleton, *Campaigns*, 216-217; Fortescue, *History of the British Army*, III, 361.

22. Graham, *Morgan*, 301-302.

23. John E. Howard's Account in *The Spirit of 'Seventy-Six The Story of the American Revolution as Told by Participants*, edited by Henry S, Commager and Richard B. Morris, 2 vols. (Indianapolis, 1958), Vol. II, 1156-1157; Graham, *Morgan*, 303.

24. Graham, *Morgan*, 303.

25. *Ibid.*, 303-305; Collins, *Autobiography*, 59.

26. Graham, *Morgan*, 304; Tarleton, *Campaigns*, 217; William Moultrie, *Memoirs of the American Revolution*, 2 vols. (New York, 1802), I, 117.

27. Johnson, *Greene*, I, 381-382; Tarleton, *Campaigns*, 217-218.

28. Howard, in *The Spirit of 'Seventy-Six*, II, 1157.

29. Graham, *Morgan*, 304-305. The hand-full of Royal Artillerists were bayoneted, sabered, or shot to the last man. Roberts, *Battle of Cowpens*, 96.

30. Tarleton, *Campaigns*, 217-218.

31. Graham, *Morgan*; 305; Bass, *Green Dragoon*, 158.

32. Bass, *Green Dragoon*, 158.

33. Johnson, *Greene*, I, 382; Graham, *Morgan*, 306.

34. Mackenzie, *Strictures*, 102.

35. Graham, *Morgan*, 307; Tarleton, *Campaigns*, 217-218.

36. Tarleton, *Campaigns*, 222.

37. Mackenzie, *Strictures*, 103.

38. Graham, *Morgan*, 307-308.

39. Morgan to Greene, Jan. 19, 1781, in Graham's *Morgan*, 310. Out of nine officers present, the 7th Fusiliers had two killed (Captain Helyar and Lieutenant Marihal), and three wounded (Major Newmarsh, and Lieutenants Harling and L'Estrange). The 1st Battalion, 71st Infantry had entered the fight with 16 officers, and it had lost two killed (Lieutenants McLeod and Chisholm) and seven wounded (Lieutenants Grant, Mackintosh, Flint, Mackenzie, Sinclair, Forbes, and Macleod). Mackenzie, *Strictures*, 111.

40. Graham, *Morgan*, 309-309. The 3 pounders had an interesting background. They had been taken from the British at Saratoga by Morgan and retaken from General Sumter by Tarleton at Blackstocks. The colors captured were those of 71st and British Legion. According to British army custom, these two units were required to henceforth wear their tunics

without facings. Rankin, "Cowpens, Prelude to Yorktown," 366.

41. Landers, *Historical Statements*, 73.

42. *Ibid.*, Ward, *War of the Revolution*, II, 762.

43. Tarleton, *Campaigns*, 221.

44. Mackenzie, *Strictures*, 115.

45. *Ibid.*, 99-100.

46. *Ibid.*, 117.

47. Landers, *Historical Statements*, 74-75.

BIBLIOGRAPHY

Anderson, Thomas. "Journal of Lt. Thomas Anderson of the Delaware Regiment," *Historical Magazine.* 2d Series.

Bass, Robert D. *The Green Dragoon.* New York, 1957.

Chastellux, Marquis de. *Travels in North America in the Years 1780, 1781, and 1782.* New York, 1928.

Clark, Walter, ed. *The State Records of North Carolina.* 16 vols. Winston-Salem and Goldsboro, 1895-1906.

Commager, Henry S. and Morris, Richard B. eds. *The Spirit of Seventy-Six—The Story of the American Revolution as Told by Participants.* 2 vols. Indianapolis, 1958.

Dictionary of American Biography. 20 vols. and Index. New York, 1928-1937.

Fortescue, John W. *A History of the British Army.* 13 vols. London, 1899-1930.

Graham, James. *The Life of General Daniel Morgan of the Virginia Line of the Army of the United States....* New York, 1859.

Higginbotham, Don. *Daniel Morgan—Revolutionary Rifleman.* Chapel Hill, 1961.

Johnson, Joseph. *Traditions and Reminiscences, Chiefly of the American Revolution in the South.* Charleston, 1851.

Johnson, William. *Sketches of the Life and Correspondence of Nathanael Greene, Major General of the Armies of the United States in the War of the Revolution.* 2 vols. Charleston, 1822.

Landers, H.L. *Historical Statements Concerning Battle of Kings Mountain and Battle of Cowpens*, South Carolina Washington, 1928.

Lee, Henry. *Memoirs of the War in the Southern Department of the United States.* New York, 1869.

Lossing, Benson J. *The Pictorial Field-Book of the Revolution.* 2 vols. New York, 1859.

Mackenzie, Roderick. *Strictures on Lt. Col. Tarleton's History "of the Campaiqns of 1780 and 1781 in the Southern Provinces of America."* London, 1785.

McGrady, Edward. *The History of South Carolina in the Revolution, 1780-1783.* New York 1902

Moultrie, William. *Memoirs of the American Revolution.* 2 vols. New York, 1802.

Myers, Theodorus B. *Cowpens Papers, Being a Correspondence of General Morgan and Prominent Actors.* Charleston, 1881.

Ramsay, David. *The History of the American Revolution.* London, 1811.

Ramsey, David. *History of the Revolution of South Carolina.* 2 vols. Trenton, 1785.

Rankin, Hugh F. "Cowpens: Prelude to Yorktown," *North Carolina Historical Review*, Vol. XXXI, No. 3. Raleigh, North Carolina.

Roberts, Kenneth L. *The Battle of Cowpens: The Great Morale Builder.* New York, 1958

Schenck, David. *North Carolinas 1780-'81, Being a History*

of the *Invasion of the Carolinas by the British Army under Lord Cornwallis*. Raleigh, 1889.

Scheer, George F. and Rankin, Hugh F. *Rebels and Redcoats.* New York, 1957.

Seymour, William. "A Journal of the Southern Expedition," *Papers of the Historical Society of Delaware*. Vol. XV. Wilmington, 1896.

Tarleton, Banastre. *A History of the Campaign of 1780 and 1781 in the Southern Provinces of North America*. Dublin, 1786.

Wallace, D. "D. Wallace's History of Union." Draper Papers. Madison Wisconsin.

Ward, Christopher. *The War of the Revolution*. 2 vols. New York, 1952.

ABOUT THE AUTHOR

Edwin Cole Bearss was born in Billings, Montana, on June 26, 1923. He grew up on his grandfather's ranch near Hardin, Montana, in the shadow of the Rosebud Mountains and within a bike ride of the Little Bighorn Battlefield. On the ranch, the E Bar S (E-S), he named the cattle for Civil War generals and battles. His favorite milk cow was Antietam.

He attended a one-room school at Sarpy, Montana, until he went to St. Johns Military Academy at Delafield, Wisconsin, in 1937. He graduated from Hardin High School and immediately joined the Marine Corps. During World War II, he was with the 3d Marine Raider Battalion and 1st Marine Division in the invasion of Guadalcanal and New Britain. Badly wounded by machine gun fire, he spent 26 months in various hospitals.

He studied at Georgetown University and received a B.S. degree in Foreign Service in 1949. He worked for three years in the Navy Hydrographic Office in Suitland, Maryland. Later, at Indiana University, he received his M.A. in history, writing his thesis on Pat Cleburne.

Bearss' National Park Service career began in 1955 at Vicksburg, Mississippi, where he was Park Historian. While he was there he did the research leading him and two friends to the long lost resting place of the Union gunboat *Cairo*. He located two forgotten forts at Grand Gulf, Mississippi. He helped get Grand Gulf made into a Mississippi State Military Monument and was the founder of the Mississippi Civil War Round Table in 1956, which later consolidated with the Jackson Civil War Round Table, a newer group.

In 1966, Bearss was transferred to Washington, DC. He became the Service's Chief Historian in November 1981, a position he held until July 1994. He served as the Director's Special Assistant for Military Sites until his retirement on October 1, 1995. Since his retirement, Bearss, through lectures, television, writing, and as a renowned battlefield guide, has continued his 50-year association with our nation's military history.

He has been the recipient of a number of awards in the

field of history and preservation: the T. Harry Williams Award; the Bruce Catton Award; the Alvin Calman Award; the Bell I. Wiley Award; and others. He was chosen Man of the Year at Vicksburg in 1963. He received the Harry S. Truman Award for Meritorious Service in the field of Civil War History. In 1964 he was chosen to become a member of the Company of Military Historians and was voted a Fellow in that organization. In 1983 he won the Department of the Interior's Distinguished Service Award, the highest award given by the department. He received a commendation from the Secretary of the Army in 1985. He is a veteran of 50 years of government service.

Bearss has done detailed studies for the National Park Service for many areas: Vicksburg; Cowpens; Pea Ridge; Wilson's Creek; the Ray House; Fort Smith; Stones River; Fort Donelson; battles around Richmond; Bighorn Canyon; Eisenhower Farm; the gold miners' route over Chilkoot Pass', LBJ Ranch; Fort Moultrie; Fort Point; William Howard Taft House; Fort Hancock; Boston Navy Yard; Herbert Hoover National Historic Site; and others.

In 1990 he was featured as a commentator on the PBS program *The Civil War*, which as of this writing is the most popular program ever to be broadcast by that network. More recently, he has appeared on the Arts & Entertainment Channel's *Civil War Journal*.

Bearss is married to the former Margie Riddle of Brandon, Mississippi. They have three children: Sara Beth, born in 1960, who has received her M.A. in history and is now editor of the *Virginia Magazine of History and Biography*; Edwin Cole, Jr., born in 1962, who retired as a gunnery sergeant in the Marine Corps and who served as an embassy guard in Bucharest and Lisbon, a drill instructor at Parris Island, South Carolina, and as Marine Corps liaison at Fort Benning, Georgia; and Mary Virginia, born in 1965, who served in the Marine Corps from 1986 to 1994. Mary Virginia's husband is a sergeant in the Corps and a veteran of Desert Storm. At present, Ed Bearss lives at 1126 South 17th Street, Arlington, Virginia 22202.